GRACE-ESTEEM
New Life in Christ

H. Eddie Fox

40,000 in print.

Reprinted 1993.

Unless otherwise indicated, all scripture quotations are taken from the Revised Standard Version of the Holy Bible.

ISBN: 0-88177-069-8

Library of Congress Catalog Card No. 88-51393

DR069

DISCIPLESHIP RESOURCES
MATERIALS FOR GROWTH IN CHRISTIAN FAITH & LIFE
— NASHVILLE, TENNESSEE —

For Mary Nell
Whose grace-full life witnesses
to the graciousness of God
through her words and deeds

❖ **TO PLACE AN ORDER** OR TO INQUIRE ABOUT
RESOURCES AND CUSTOMER ACCOUNTS, CONTACT:

> DISCIPLESHIP RESOURCES DISTRIBUTION CENTER
> P.O. BOX 6996
> ALPHARETTA, GEORGIA 30239-6996
>
> TEL: (800) 685-4370
>
> FAX: (404) 442-5114

❖ **FOR EDITORIAL INQUIRIES** AND RIGHTS AND
PERMISSIONS REQUESTS, CONTACT:

> DISCIPLESHIP RESOURCES EDITORIAL OFFICES
> P.O. BOX 840
> NASHVILLE, TENNESSEE 37202-0840
>
> TEL: (615) 340-7068

CONTENTS

INTRODUCTION

For by grace you have been saved through faith;
And this is not your own doing, it is the gift of
God.

Ephesians 2:8

The greatest need of any person is to be known and
loved. The cry is strong; the human desire is deep.
"I want to be somebody. I want my life to count."
Closely related to the feeling of worth is the perception
of who we are. When we esteem something or someone, we highly value it or the person. To esteem
ourselves is to have high regard for ourselves. Many of
the problems in human relations stem from a person's
lack of self-esteem.

Many books deal with personal esteem. This book is
deeply personal, but it contends that our worth and
value is given. We are called not to muster it up within
ourselves, but to receive the gift given to us, a gift of
the grace of God in Jesus Christ. God has declared our
value.

Our value is not rooted in self-esteem, based only in

ourselves. Our value is discovered in *grace*, which is rooted in the greatness and graciousness of God.

A dot on the map

The incredibly beautiful South Pacific kingdom of Tonga consists of many small islands which are populated by about 100,000 people. Tonga is located near the international dateline and is the place that sees the earliest rising of the sun of each new day. I was there in December 1977 to speak at the South Pacific Youth Convention of The Methodist Church. I have never heard such singing and witnessed such beautiful dances. As the people lifted their voices in beautiful harmony, the ocean and the wind surged through the coconut palms which seemed to join in the praise of the Almighty God.

On the last Sunday of the convention, more than 2,500 people gathered in the church to worship, including the king, queen, and royal family of Tonga. To declare the good news of Jesus Christ and to share in that worship service was one of my greatest joys.

After the worship service, the word came that His Majesty King Taufa'ahau Tupou IV desired that I visit his family at their home. As we were received into the king's library, he asked, "You are from the United States?"

"Yes, Your Majesty."

"Where is your home?"

"Nashville, Tennessee."

One of the sons of the king said, "Nashville—home of bluegrass music."

His Majesty the King was not content with the information. He picked up a world atlas, turned to the southeastern section of the United States, and found Tennessee. He stated that he had visited Atlanta, Georgia and Emory University. I pointed out that it is only 200 miles from Nashville to Atlanta. I was surprised when His Majesty said, "I want to ask you a question. I have been looking at this map of Georgia, north to south and east to west. Would you please show me where Plains, Georgia is?"

I looked at his map and Plains was not on it. "Your Majesty, Plains is right there—12 miles from Americus, not very far from Albany and Columbus." I took my pen and made a little dot on the king's map.

When I returned home I wrote to President Carter, "Dear Mr. President, I have done for you a great service. You will be glad to know that your dot is now on the 'king's map,'" and I related the above story. A letter came from an assistant to the president, "The president is grateful for the service you have rendered on his behalf." A few years later I had the opportunity to tell President and Mrs. Carter personally that their "dot" was on the king's map.

My dot and your dot are on the king's map, not in Tonga but on the map of the Sovereign ruler of all life. To have our dot on the Lord's map means that we are known, loved, and valued. We are somebody. The Bible speaks of this worth: "You are now the people of God, who once were not (God's) people; outside (God's) mercy once, you have now received (God's) mercy" (1 Peter 2:10, NEB).

We are creatures of great worth because we receive God's mercy and grace. The message of the Christian faith is that, though once you may have felt you were a nobody, in God's grace and love you are now somebody. You are even a royal people, for you are the people of God (1 Peter 2:9-10).

The greatest need for you and me is a regular encounter in our experience with the God of grace revealed in Jesus Christ. It is in the experience of this grace—the unmerited, unearned, undeserved love of a self-sacrificing God—that we come to a new life in Christ. The old song declared, "You're nobody till somebody loves you." Well, somebody has loved us and does love us. This somebody is God. Our worth is not constituted by the job we do. We are not determined by where we live. We are not equated with our achievement scores. Our value is not rooted in the school we attended. Our worth is not in who we are but in who God is.

God's love makes it possible to know we are valued. We cannot put ourselves down or debase ourselves. We can know our true worth because we are the children of God. Our esteem is rooted in the amazing grace of God. Our esteem is grace-esteem.

Life itself is by *grace,* not of ourselves; it is the gift of God. The Good News is the grace of the Lord Jesus

Christ. The story of the New Testament is the story of the primacy of grace.

The tendency of humankind is to look inward instead of outward to discover our value. We want to raise our self-esteem by self-effort and self-realization. This leaves us feeling hopeless and helpless. Albert Outler points out that the human condition is "defeating in the sense that it defeats the point of self-realization. The human aim of self-realization is self-defeating because it does not lead to self-realization. But the gospel of grace does!" (from a lecture on February 25, 1986; Nashville, TN). Therefore, our hope is in grace. Self-help salvation will not work. Too many people have been offered false hopes and false remedies for our needs. Too often we are told "Do it yourself," but we know we are not adequate. Even though we stamp "OK" on ourselves, there is a deeper need within us. We are created in a shape to receive grace. The scripture makes it perfectly clear, "For it is by God's grace you are saved, through trusting him; it is not your own doing. It is God's gift" (Ephesians 2:8, NEB).

Let us celebrate the grace of God and witness to this grace revealed in Jesus Christ. God's grace bestows dignity on each person! We are invited to experience this amazing grace in our lives so that we will know the fullness of GRACE-ESTEEM.

Chapter I
GRACIOUS GOD

Grace-esteem is rooted in the God of grace and glory who is revealed in Jesus Christ. This goodness and graciousness of God is revealed constantly and consistently in the creating, caring, sustaining, and redeeming activity of God.

Creation

The graceful activity of God is seen in creation. God creates the heavens and earth. God's spirit moves across the waters, and the spoken word of God brings forth light. The dry land appears, and the earth springs forth in fruit. All living creatures are created by God. God sees all creation and pronounces it good.

God creates the human being in the very image of God. God pronounces that male and female are "very good." The grace of God is seen in the goodness of God's creation. Stamped on male and female are the words "in the image of God."

In creation there is harmony and order between God and humankind, humankind and nature, and with nature itself. There is no hint of slavery or bond-

1

age in creation, such as man over woman or woman over man. There is mutual harmony and helpfulness in the creative order as the sovereign rule of grace is established. Creation is good because of the graciousness of God.

Reality of sin

Humankind rebels against the reign of God. Adam and Eve turn away to follow their own passions and desires and attempt to hide from God. This rebellion against God results in estrangement and bondage. Sin disfigures the image of God in human beings. Sin blurs, scars, distorts, and tarnishes the "imago dei." The divine image is radically damaged by the effect of sin. Since the intimate relationship between humankind and God is being shattered, the result is separation, self-deception, self-captivity. Humankind is enslaved in the bondage of death.

This flaw is universal. Sin contaminates all of life and existence. It is like a malignant disease which destroys and corrupts the whole of humankind. All are infected by this spiritual sickness. The scripture makes clear this universality of sin:

> There is no one who is righteous, no one who understands, or who seeks for God. All men have turned away from God; they have all gone wrong; No one does what is good, not even one.
> (Romans 3:10-12, TEV)

`All are under the power and dominion of sin (Romans

3:9). Clearly we are all sinners so that this broken relationship penetrates the very core of our existence. Paul describes the human condition as one unto death, bondage, slavery, and helplessness.

Wesley describes the human condition as utterly destitute, with the image of God so disfigured, marred, and obliterated that humankind is unable to redeem itself. In fact, humankind is so captive that we are not free to choose whether or not to sin. The bondage is so complete that we are unable to rescue ourselves. Sin is so radically rooted in human nature that to break its dominion and power we need radical salvation. The reality is that we do not have the power to not sin. Therefore, God helps us, which is the point of grace. Only the grace of God and divine love can take away our "bent to sinning" (*The United Methodist Hymnal*, 384).

Radical grace

The love of God pursues men and women even when they turn away and hide from God. God seeks us long before we seek God. God does not give up the intent to be in a whole and right relationship with creation. The vision is not abandoned.

The message of the Bible is one of the persistent and patient grace of God in pursuit of humankind. The message of the prophet Hosea declares this grace of God. Hosea is a prophet of Israel who, through his own experience, discovers the grace of God. His message is one of stern judgment and righteousness.

Hosea and his wife Gomer have three children. The

3

first son is named Jezreel. When the people of Israel see the child they remember the story. Jezreel is a place where the Israelites knew defeat in their history. The prophet's message rings within them, "Your sin means that you are defeated." The second child is named "Not Pitied." Again, the people remember the message, "You are sinners and because of your transgression God will 'not pity' you any longer." The message is stern and hard. What does the third child feel when his name is called "Not My People"? This is the strongest word from the prophet. You are transgressors of the law of the Lord. Because of this sin you have forfeited your call as the chosen people of God. In fact, the prophet thundered, "You are 'not my people' says the Lord God." It is a message of doom.

About this time in the prophet's life, his wife Gomer leaves him and willfully resumes a life of prostitution. It is devastating to the prophet. The pain of the separation is so intense that it is unbearable. The prophet discovers that he still loves his wife, and he is hurt to see her suffering. This reality leads him to discover that God does not give up on chosen people. Hosea glimpses the grace of God which expresses a love that will not let us go. His message is recharged, and he preaches that this grace "will heal their faithlessness;" and "will love them freely" (Hosea 14:4).

The song of the psalmist reminds us that surely the goodness and mercy (the graciousness) of God will follow us all the days of our lives. The psalmist reminds us that it is futile to try to get away from God. Wherever we go, God is there following us all of our days.

4

Grace disclosed

This grace of God is ultimately and uniquely disclosed in Jesus Christ. The life of Jesus reveals this persistent, divine love. Jesus seeks out the weak, the vulnerable, the outcast, the lonely, the distraught, and the despised. He eats with those least likely to seek him. He makes it clear that his ministry is to seek and to save the lost. He expresses love to those who are least likely to expect it. By expressing this grace to such people, Jesus encounters trouble with others who cannot understand grace.

The picture of a God who is like a landowner who pays all the workers the same at the end of the day, regardless of how long they worked, is radical. We do not earn such a gift, but it is given by the sovereign God. Grace is a problem for some people in the same way that the older son is upset with the father and mother for having a big celebration when the young "prodigal son" comes home. Yet the message of Jesus continually points to this grace. He declares that a new age has dawned, a new age of grace. He tells stories which point to this gracious heart of God. Jesus says that if a neighbor eventually will answer a knock on the door in the middle of the night, how much more God acts in love and grace toward God's children. We can be sure of God's grace to us!

The full revelation of this grace is seen in the dying and rising of Jesus Christ. The cross reveals the nature of God. When we stand beneath the cross of Jesus and look up at the face of Jesus, we discover the perfect love and amazing grace of God. We are as astounded as Charles Wesley who exclaimed:

> Amazing love! How can it be
> that thou, my Lord, shouldst die for me?
> (*The United Methodist Hymnal,* 363)

On the cross, we see the full expression of the God who "loves the world so much." Jesus Christ is not just any person; Jesus Christ is God (incarnate). Our sin breaks the heart of God. In the story of the cross we see the result of human sin as we witness the death of the finest and purest life that ever lived. Yet God in Jesus reaches out with the word of forgiveness and reconciliation. The cross makes possible our being reconciled with God. Its purpose is not to reconcile God to us but to reconcile the world, including you and me, to God. "God was in Christ reconciling the world to himself" (2 Corinthians 5:19, NEB). The cross reveals the heart of God; it is not an event designed to change the mind of God. It is grace to redeem and restore the image of God in humankind and creation. Here is the apex of God's love for all persons.

Jesus' death strikes a mortal blow to sin and death. When Jesus is lifted on the cross and then raised from the dead, the power of sin and death is shattered. Jesus meets death, but it is death that is defeated. When Jesus comes forth from the empty tomb, he opens the door for our salvation. He dies and rises to set us free. The very fiber of the universe is changed. God in Christ acts to liberate us and to restore the divine order of creation. God's grace makes it possible to be free from the bondage and slavery of sin. The incredible word rises and declares God's yes to the world. Christ Jesus "is the YES pronounced upon God's promises, every one of them" (2 Corinthians 1:20, NEB).

When Charles Wesley witnessed this love, he declared:

> Love divine, all loves excelling;
> > Joy of heaven to earth come down.
> Fix in us thy humble dwelling;
> > All thy faithful mercies crown!
> Jesus, thou art all compassion,
> > Pure unbounded love thou art;
> > visit us with thy salvation;
> > enter every trembling heart.
> (*The United Methodist Hymnal*, 384)

Grace comes to us

The grace of God comes to us, and we are not left alone. For example, a picture of two little twin boys appeared in a newspaper. They were completely bald. The story told that one of the twins had leukemia and was taking chemotherapy as treatment. This medicine resulted in the loss of his hair. Some children at school made fun of him and teased him about his lack of hair. In a cruel way, they thought he looked funny. This was more than the other twin brother could take. So, he had his head shaved so that he was exactly like his brother! Now their peers could laugh at both of them. He could not stand for his brother to be alone. This story illustrates the message of the Christian faith. God, Immanuel, has come to us. God's love takes upon Godself our condition to redeem us. We are not alone. There is no greater love than this. It is grace, all graces excelling!

Redemption is possible

Several years ago, "Tie a Yellow Ribbon 'Round the Old Oak Tree" was a popular song. Much earlier, there was a legendary story that circulated and was the basis of the song. The popularity of the song over the years indicates how the story touches our human emotions.

A young son leaves home and lives a life that results in his being imprisoned. As the time comes for him to be released, he writes his father and mother a letter in which he tells them that he knows that he has brought shame to them and the family. He states that he would understand if they did not want him to come back home. The letter then tells them that on a particular day he is planning to be on the train back to their hometown. Because the train goes by the family home, the boy writes his mother and father, "If you want me to come home, tie a yellow ribbon 'round the old oak tree behind the house." The day arrives and the boy's heart is pounding. Finally, he relates his story to the man sitting next to him on the train. He points out that they are almost there and that he is unable to look for himself. He requests that the stranger look for him. As the train rounds the bend, the man lifts the boy's face and declares, "Look, boy, look! There's a yellow ribbon on every limb!"

This story touches any person who knows what it is like to have a broken relationship restored. We are moved by knowing a love that forgives us even when we do not deserve it. We have all received a "yellow ribbon" of grace.

God's grace makes this possible! In Jesus Christ's life, death, and resurrection, God has acted to make possible our being "put right" with God. God's grace makes possible the recovery of God's original design for God's children and the recovery of God's design for all of space, time, and the universe.

This redemption is rooted in the suffering, dying, and rising love of God. Jesus' way was the way of the cross, and God raised him from the dead. Christ has died and risen to break the bondage and the yoke of sin. The power of evil is broken, and sin has no right to control us as individuals, churches, societies, or nations. It is no wonder we exclaim in song with Wesley:

> O for a thousand tongues to sing
> my great redeemer's praise
> the glories of my God and King,
> The *triumphs* of His grace.
> (*The United Methodist Hymnal,* 57)

In the midsection of the United States, we recently experienced more than four months without rain. As people watched their crops dry up and the grass become parched, we realized how dependent we are on the rain to water the earth.

Without the grace of God, our lives are empty, dry,

9

and parched. We cannot live. But the self-disclosure of God reveals the God of grace and glory. We are given the possibility of redemption through the graciousness of God in Jesus Christ. This grace can be for all of us saving grace.

Questions for discussion

1. Have you experienced separation? How did you feel when someone you loved left you? Did you want to do something to restore the relationship, to bring them back?

   When have you hurt to see another suffering? What did you want to do for that person? How do you understand God's love for us during these experiences?

2. When have you known unexpected love in your own life from friends or loved ones? When have you experienced the surprise of God's love?

3. Can you think of a time when an undeserving person received love from others? (It may be that later you rejoiced, but perhaps your first reaction to a situation was more negative.)

4. When have you given or expressed radical love for someone? What was your motivation?

5. When have you known or experienced the restoration of a broken relationship? With another person? With God?

Chapter II
SAVING GRACE

"Have you heard the latest word?" the stranger asked me as we met in the corridor of the Dallas-Fort Worth International Airport.

"I don't know if it's the latest word or not, but it has not changed. Let's go find out," was my reply.

The two of us went into a room and watched television. We saw that the situation was just as it was earlier. I boarded the plane to travel on to Nashville, and the flight attendant asked, "Have you heard recently?"

"Yes! It's just the same as before."

Upon arrival in Nashville, I quickly rushed to see if there were any new developments. There was no change. That evening as I was watching television, there was suddenly an interruption of the regular programming. Immediately, I was watching the drama in Texas. I called my wife to come, "Hurry! Hurry! Look, they're getting her out of the well."

With tears running down my face, I watched as a little girl was lifted out of a well where she had been trapped for hours and days. I saw men wearing hard hats with rock dust all over their faces and women whose eyes were tired from lack of sleep, all rejoicing because this beautiful little girl was rescued alive. I knew that these people had been working throughout the day and night over machines with diamond-studded bits, drilling through solid rock to create an opening through which the little girl was set free. Millions of people around the entire world witnessed the scene through television. The next day newspapers exclaimed in headlines, "The Little Girl in the Well Is Alive" and "Jessica Saved." It is no cliché. New life is possible and real. Our hearts are gladdened. It is good news. Everywhere people are rejoicing, and even the angels sing the glad tidings.

The message of the Christian faith is good news! This is the meaning of the Greek word *evangel*. It is rooted in the image of the marathon runner who races back from the battle with the word of victory. Coming to the crest of the hill, with lungs bursting and bathed in perspiration, the herald declares that "victory is ours." Paul says that the feet of the messengers of good news are welcome (Romans 10:15)!

Core of the message

The human spirit cries out, "Have you heard? Do you know any new word?"

"Yes," we answer. "We have heard. God has acted in grace through the Lord Jesus Christ so that all who receive him are forgiven of their sins." This is the core of the gospel message. This is the very essence, the center of God's grace. God has come to redeem humankind and all of creation. The little girl is rescued from the well, and similarly the grace of God shatters

12

the power of evil and makes possible our freedom from the bondage and slavery of sin.

In Christ everything is different. The early disciples declared that a new age had come. The powers of darkness no longer hold dominion over creation. Sin, evil, and death are conquered. A way of deliverance is coming. The human reach is never long enough. The wonderful news is that God's grace reaches out to us. The human reach results in self-defeat, the collapse upon ourselves, others, and creation. The extension of grace makes possible our redemption, reconciliation, and restoration. Such an act results in the birth and growth of grace-esteem in our lives. Through grace we are enabled to live a life of meaning and hope. By grace it is possible for us to live a life that counts.

Salvation by our own moral effort is not a productive human option. We cannot achieve our redemption. Even though we have had almost a century of the notion of human achievement on human exertion alone, we are only now recognizing its essential futility. We are once again confessing our need for help beyond ourselves. In this quest, people turn to magic, astrology, and self-discovery. The newest self-help, self-discovery book becomes a best-seller in just a matter of weeks. Yet the message is clear and definite—we cannot set ourselves free by our own effort. "For it is by (God's) grace you are saved, through trusting him; it is not your own doing. It is God's gift" (Ephesians 2:8, NEB). "Now that we have been put right with God through faith, we have peace with God through our Lord Jesus Christ. He has brought us, by faith, into this experience of God's grace, in which we now live" (Romans 5:1-2, TEV).

No one needs to perish. No one needs to live a wasted life. Grace makes it possible that all people may be redeemed. Paul writes that the message of Jesus is "nonsense to those who are *being lost;* but for us who are *being saved,* it is God's power" (1 Corinthians 1:18, TEV). Note that the dividing line is between those who are *being* lost or *being* saved. Paul wants it clear that, indeed, no one need perish. Nothing is final until the end of time.

See and enter the kingdom

By God's grace we see and enter into the kingdom of God. Jesus himself makes that very clear to a religious leader named Nicodemus, when speaking to him about the necessity of the new birth. So often Jesus takes very familiar, natural processes to open up spiritual understanding. He talks about the seed, flowers, sheep, coins, sons and daughters, fathers and mothers, employers, wages, fish, boats, wind, pearls, sunrises, and sunsets. Through these familiar images, he opens vistas of the kingdom of God. Here again he takes that which is familiar—birth—and enables people to catch a glimpse of the reign of grace.

This record is the only story in which we have Jesus using the phrase, "You must be born again." He speaks to a religious leader! Jesus did not say this to Andrew, Simon Peter, Mary Magdalene, or Zacchaeus.

Only to Nicodemus did he use these words. Nicodemus is perplexed by Jesus' words, but Jesus insists that you must be born again. Why do you suppose that Jesus said it to a religious leader? Could it be that religious people often feel in charge of their own salvation? Religious leaders feel that they can handle matters of ultimate importance.

Jesus is making it clear to Nicodemus that you cannot see and enter this kingdom of God through your own strength and merit any more than you can give birth to yourself. In fact, no person can give birth to oneself! It does not matter if you are a king or a queen, prince or princess, bishop or president, you cannot bear yourself. For the person who says, "I didn't ask to be born," let's be clear—no person controls his/her entrance into this world. Birth is a gift. Salvation is made possible as a gift. (I must note here that there is a distinct difference between the physical birth and the "New Birth" at this point. We shall see later that the human response made possible by grace needs to be exercised in faith.)

In the process of birth, we can see the Holy Spirit at work as the agent of grace. Our daughter was born on January 1. Born twenty-eight minutes after midnight, she was a New Year's baby. But we missed a tax deduction by less than one half-hour. This birthday is very important to us, as we celebrate it. But this was not the beginning or the ending of this beautiful life. There was much that happened before—love, commitment, relationship, conception, development, growth, and then birth!

Before birth

The period prior to our birth is of great importance to our health and vitality for our entire life! Occasionally I meet someone who says, "I grew up in the church, but when I was thirty-two years old I met the Lord. Everything that happened previously was insignificant." I say, "Oh no, that is your spiritual prenatal time." Wesley calls this prevenient grace, that is, grace which "goes before." This grace means that before we know God, God knows us. Before we love, God loves. This grace is *for all.* It is not for the select or elite; grace is given to the whole human race because God loves every one of us. This affects how I feel about myself and others. It is an important ingredient of grace-esteem.

It is true that conversion is like birth—we cannot earn it. We are helpless, but we are not hopeless. Grace has been given, which makes it possible for us to receive life itself. This grace at God's initiative is working in our lives. Wesley speaks of salvation as

the entire work of God, from the first dawning of grace in the soul till it is consummated in glory. ... it will include all that is wrought in the soul by what is frequently termed "natural conscience," but more properly, "preventing grace"; all the "drawings" of "the Father," the desires after God, which, if we yield to them, increase more and more; all that "light" wherewith the Son of God "enlighteneth everyone that cometh into the world," showing every man "to do justly, to love mercy and to walk humbly with his God"; all the convictions which his spirit from time to time work in every child of man.[1]

For Wesley, the original righteousness in creation is so badly blurred and disfigured that only by this grace given to all and for all is redemption possible. The spirit as an agent of grace nudges us toward God. It awakens us to the possibility of salvation. It disturbs us and convinces us of our need for God. It helps us be aware of beauty. It creates in us a thirst for God. This grace entices us and leads us toward God. This grace apprehends us as we run away from God. It illuminates scripture and stimulates our desire to know and love God.

This grace of God reminds us that we are totally dependent on God for salvation. Similar to physical birth, one can experience the New Birth by grace alone and not by any person's own merit or achievement. But the Second Birth is distinctive from the physical birth in that we are called to accept or respond to this gift. The Spirit places in each person the desire to aim for the good.

This grace leads us toward the response of faith. But not everyone responds to this grace in faith. Grace must be received, accepted, and appropriated for us to experience its transforming power.

Wesley emphasized that this grace given to all is not irresistible. If grace were irresistible, then we would not be made in the image of God. We would be robots. As it is, however, we have the live option of responding to the grace of God. Some may decide to come and some may not. This prevenient grace, which is offered to all and enables each person to turn to God, makes all people responsible for their choices.

> God makes it possible but doesn't enforce it. Each human response to God's grace is, therefore, truly that person's own response. We are not objects of divine manipulation. Yet we can only make such a response because God's prevenient grace has made it possible. If we respond positively and are saved, we have no credit to claim for ourselves. Our response was only possible because of God's grace. If we reject and are lost, however, we have nothing to complain about.[2]

It is your decision—God's grace makes it possible.

At birth

In birth a baby picks up the option to live. In the New Birth, we accept, receive, and respond in trust to the grace offered. We pick up the option to live, truly live. We rejoice in the promise that to "all who did receive him, to those who have yielded him their allegiance, he gave the right to become children of God" (John 1:12, NEB). Under the influence of this gift of grace, we are called to repentance and faith. The heart of the New Testament message is that while we are still estranged, God loves us. "We see sin not as a crime against law but as a crime against love. To be sure, in sin, we break God's law, but more important, we break

18

God's heart. We may atone for a broken law, but how do we atone for a broken heart?"[3]

Charles Wesley answers such a question by declaring:

> Plenteous Grace with thee is found.
> Grace to cover all my sin.
> Let the healing streams abound;
> Make and keep me pure within.
> Thou of Life the fountain art;
>   freely let me take of thee.
> Spring thou up within my heart;
>   rise to all eternity.
> (*The United Methodist Hymnal*, 479)

This transforming grace involves our cooperating with grace. We accept this gift of life. The human response is that of trust. In fact, Wesley says that faith is the condition of justification. "None is justified but he that believes; without faith no one is justified. . . . In other words: no one is justified till he believes; every man when he believes is justified."[4]

What is the content of the response of faith? Faith involves our accepting that God has accepted us. It is trusting that God has forgiven us. It is receiving the pardon that is offered us. It is opening our life to the grace given us. It is believing that this new life is possible for me. It is affirming that Jesus' death and resurrection makes the difference between death and life for me.

Indeed, it is an awesome mystery, experienced on a trip to the beautiful island of Fiji, when I discovered anew the wonderful power of God's amazing grace.

Upon arrival in Savu Savu, there was a traditional welcome given to me. At an appropriate moment, one of the elders of the church came forward and extended to me the Tabua. The Tabua, a whale's tooth, is a very special treasure for the Fijian people. It is a sign of peace, friendship, and reconciliation. When it is offered by a Fijian and accepted by another person, then no wall or enmity can exist between them. In some of the churches one will see the Tabua hanging beside or under the cross.

This symbol clearly illustrates how we are one with God by the shedding of the blood of Christ for the sins of all humankind. When the gift of grace is received and appropriated in faith, we experience forgiveness. There is no wall of separation between God and creature and creation. It is like being born. We come to life.

Process of birth

This process of new birth may vary according to the way God has made us. When we were expecting our daughter to be born, we did not think she would ever arrive. We waited and waited and, finally, she was born. For our twin sons, there was no delay in their birth; they were born three minutes apart on Labor Day. They did not tarry at all. Quickly we arrived at the hospital, and very quickly they were born. If you were to ask me which child is more alive the daughter or the sons, I would suggest that you ask crazy questions. Yet we meet people who are hung up on the speed of the New Birth. For some, the New Birth seems instantaneous. They know a place, a spot, and a time when they were born. Yet for others, new birth seems less dramatic.

Some of the most interesting people to watch on television are the weather forecasters. They have a tough job. Many times they do not have much news to report, but they are required to make it seem interesting. So, they have graphs, charts, and figures to flash at us. The display is impressive. About the only figure or graph I understand is the one that says "sunrise tomorrow at 6:23 A.M." I often wonder how they know that. How do they decide when the sun comes up? Is it when the orange ball appears just on the horizon? Is it when the first ray of sun streaks across the sky? Is it when a light meter registers so much? In the Great Smoky Mountains in Southern Appalachia the time of sunrise is determined by which mountain you are on, or on which side of the mountain you are living. But some people never see the sunrise; they simply get up in the morning and start walking around.

So it is in the experience of coming to the newness of life. Some experiences are like the dramatic encounter on the road to Damascus when Paul was suddenly blinded by a bright light and confronted by the spoken word from God. Other experiences are like those persons who are walking to Emmaus. They are lonely and a stranger joins them. Only when they have the blessing and break the bread, do they realize that the one in their presence is the Lord.

The threshold of response will vary according to the way the Creator has made us. And we are not all alike. The Creator has given us different personalities and

21

temperaments. Even the nursery rhymes acknowledge this:

> Jack Sprat could eat no fat,
>> His wife could eat no lean;
> And so between them both,
>> they licked the platter clean.[5]

We are grateful that God allows us to respond faithfully in keeping with the way we are made.

We must not become so enamored with the steps of the process that we miss the reality of the experience. Our New Birth involves a long process. First comes the experience before birth and then birth itself. We can never isolate any of the experiences of faith from the ongoing life of grace. Wesley records in his journal that on May 24, 1738 at about a quarter before 9:00, "I felt my heart strangely warmed." Even though Wesley gives a specific time, it is possible only to understand his experience of faith in light of his journey before and after this moment at Aldersgate. In fact, there were tremendous turnings and decisions made in his life over a two-year period before and after his Aldersgate experience.

Joy of birth

Most of the time there is great joy whenever a child is born. We still celebrate January 1 and September 5 at our house. To receive the gift of grace and forgiveness in Christ and to respond in repentance and trust is also an experience of great joy. We are put right or justified.

Dikaioun is the Greek word which is translated as "to justify." Barclay points out that this word does not mean to make someone something, but to treat, reckon or to account someone as something. Dunnam expands "that although we are utterly guilty before God, we are treated and accounted by grace as innocent."[6] To be put right before God is the meaning of grace-esteem. We are treated as if we are somebody. It is a cause for great rejoicing.

Jesus by his dying and rising shatters the dominion of sin. His sacrifice and the shedding of his blood atones for my sins and the sins of the whole world. Charles Wesley breaks into praise when he sees a power available which can set us free and make us clean and new.

> He breaks the power of cancelled sin.
> He sets the prisoner free.
> His blood can make the foulest clean.
> His blood availed for me.
> (*The United Methodist Hymnal*, 57)

We break into joy and ecstasy as we continue in song with Wesley:

> And can it be that I should gain
> An interest in the Saviour's blood?
> Died he for me, who caused his pain?
> For me, who him to death pursued?
> Amazing love! How can it be
> that thou my Lord shouldst die for me?
> (*The United Methodist Hymnal*, 363)

This hymn is probably the greatest hymn sung by

23

the company of Methodism all over the world. It is sung by Abel and Freda Hendricks, from South Africa. This Methodist pastor and his wife, labeled "coloured" by their government, know what it means to be literally imprisoned as followers of Christ. Abel has been made to stand for hours in prison and suffer humiliation at the hands of his accusers. Because of the enslavement of his people by the apartheid government in South Africa, he knows what it is like to be in prison all the time—sometimes in jail and sometimes by discrimination. The slavery of apartheid imprisons Abel and Freda, and the people of their country are oppressed together.

Let us remember the face of Abel and Freda as we sing the words of Wesley:

> Long my imprisoned spirit lay;
>> fast bound in sin and nature's night;
> Thine *eye* diffused a quickening ray;
> I woke, the dungeon flamed with light;
> *My chains fell off,*
> My heart was free.
> I rose, went forth, and followed thee.

The voices rise in a crescendo as we all sing:

> No condemnation now I dread;
>> Jesus, and all in him, is mine;
>> alive in him, my living Head,
>> and clothed in righteousness divine,
>> bold I approach th'eternal throne,
> And claim the crown, through Christ
>> my own.
> (*The United Methodist Hymnal,* 363)

By God's grace we are born to a *new life*. We are granted grace-esteem. But, the journey is not over when we are born. By God's grace it is possible to grow up in grace.

Questions for discussion

1. When have you felt in bondage, in prison, by a situation, action, or thought? How have you experienced new life in Christ out of that situation?

   Do you know of someone who is currently going through a difficult time of bondage? In addition to your prayers for them, how might you witness to God's saving grace?

2. Was your new birth experience more like the Damascus Road or the Emmaus Road experience? Reflect and explain.

3. In what specific ways do you continue to experience the *process* of new birth?

4. Reflect on your faith journey. How did you experience "prenatal" care and nurturing?

Chapter III

GROWING GRACE

O to *grace* how great a debtor
   daily I'm constrained to be.
Let thy goodness like a fetter
   bind my wandering heart to thee.
   (*The United Methodist Hymnal*, 400)

Grace-esteem means that all of life is given by the grace of God. The core of it is:

> When anyone is united to Christ, there is a new world; the old order has gone, and a new order has already begun.

> (2 Corinthians 5:17, NEB)

We have already focused on the reality that by God's grace the new life is possible. The Holy Spirit as the agent of grace makes possible our being born again. But let's be clear that the New Birth is not the end of our conversion. If it is an end, it is the front end!

In a moment of time, birth takes place physically. But so much takes place before and after the recorded moment. After birth, there is the process of growth. The dynamic of growth is made possible by the dynamic of grace.

For John Wesley, the New Birth involves real as well as relative change.[1] This New Birth involves a new relationship with God. We are put right. We are forgiven. God does not remember our sins any more. They are removed as far as the east is from the west. There is no wall of separation and brokenness between God and humankind as a result of our being born again. Justification, being put right with God, is what God does for us. The new relationship is established.

Born to grow

For Wesley there is a *real change*. There is New Birth and new life. Wesley preaches:

> From the time of our being "born again" the gradual work of sanctification takes place. . . . we are more and more alive to God. We go on from *grace to grace* [emphasis added], while we are careful to "abstain from all appearance of evil," and are "zealous of good works," "as we have opportunity, doing good to all men"; while we walk in all his ordinances blameless, therein worshipping him in spirit and in truth; while we take up our cross and deny ourselves *every* pleasure that does not lead us to God.[2]

In physical birth we pass from the womb into the world outside, and outside we continue to grow and mature. We are born to grow, and this New Birth effects a *real* change in us. The sanctifying grace is what Christ does *in us*, enabling us to grow into his likeness. We are being transformed into Christ-likeness. The restoration of the divine image takes place by the means of grace and more grace.

We are often aware of the growth in the children who are a part of our lives. When our children were small, there were times when months would pass before they could see their grandparents. Maybe even a year or more would go by before they would see some great-aunt or great-uncle. The reaction was always the same, "My, how these children have grown. Look at them! I can't believe my eyes! Why, you were just this high last time, and now look at you. Wow!" We celebrated the growth that had taken place.

In the home of my wife's aunt, there is a board beside a door in an upstairs bedroom which has many dates and lines on it. There are lines with the names of Mary Nell and her brothers which indicate their height on a particular date. We enjoyed standing our children beside the board and measuring them against the height of their mother at the same age. Growth is important, so we take stock of it in our lives.

The energy and the dynamic for growth is released within our bodies. Thus we have much to do with our growth, health, and vitality. We recognize that we cannot give life to ourselves and that there are "givens" in our physical growth. Yet, we also know that we can stunt our growth. Our strength and stamina have much to do with how we treat our bodies.

Need for exercise

The New Birth is the entrance into the kingdom by grace. Life in the kingdom of grace requires a particular form of exercise. We are given the grace and strength to exercise. Today many people seek diligently to be physically fit. Some people are obsessed with having the body fit and strong. Jesus also has much to say about "fitness" in the kingdom. We are challenged to "get into shape." Remember that we are created in the shape and image of God. Therefore, we are challenged to become increasingly like the divine image originally created in humankind. By grace we are enabled to become increasingly transformed into the image revealed in Jesus Christ. We are challenged to "work out."

> You must work out your own salvation in fear and trembling; for it is God who works in you, inspiring both the will and deed, for his own chosen purpose.
>
> (Philippians 2:12-13, NEB)

At about fifteen years of age, our sons were six feet tall and weighed 140 pounds when wet. They could almost walk through the crack in the door when it was closed!

Since they were so skinny, they wanted muscles. They visited a strength and conditioning coach at a university in Nashville to ask if he was willing to help them learn to lift weights. He said that he would be glad to help. "You come three days a week, two hours

30

each time, and I'll show you what to do," the coach said. "By the way, the first time you miss, you're out." Now that is a very tough commitment. "Come, work, and you will develop muscles." I remember watching my sons as they perspired and lifted weights. They were determined. They wanted strong muscles. They challenged me, "Dad, why don't you lift weights?"

"I do," I replied, "every time I stand up."

Days passed, and they continued to spend hours each week "working out." Fat content was replaced by muscles.

After a few days they came home with a diet given to them by their coach. The coach made it clear that what you eat has a lot to do with the muscles and strength you develop. The diet included liver! We began eating liver at least once a week. Muscles and strength are related to exercise and diet.

Paul challenged Timothy to "keep [himself] in training for a godly life. Physical exercise has some value in it, but spiritual exercise is valuable in every way, because it promises life both for now and for the future" (1 Timothy 4:7-8, TEV).

There is no room for couch-potato Christians. That is, we should not take a chair and merely sit. A "couch potato" is the person who admits coming home, sitting down, watching television, and eating junk food. Growing strong and fit demands regular exercise and good nutrition.

Commitment

Paul witnesses to the commitment to live the life of Christian discipleship: "All I can say is this: forgetting what is behind me, and reaching out for that which lies ahead, I press towards the goal to win the prize which is God's call to the life above, in Christ Jesus" (Philippians 3:13-14, NEB). Growth in the Christian life is neither accidental nor magical. It requires commitment to disciplined living. Note the words of Paul as he describes this journey of discipleship—forgetting, reaching, pressing, winning—strong words demanding our full allegiance and loyalty. There are no part-time Christians. Paul writes to the Corinthians and calls them to this commitment:

> Run, then, in such a way as to win the prize. Every athlete in training submits to strict discipline; . . . in order to be crowned with a wreath that will not last; but we do it for one that will last forever. That is why I run straight for the finish line.
>
> (1 Corinthians 9:24-26, TEV)

This call to commitment seems to be out of place for much of our world.

Our day does not easily use the word *commitment*. Much of Western society is an "instant society." Whatever we want, we want it now. We eat instant potatoes, pudding, and cereal. We drink instant tea and coffee. We live in a world of condensed books, abridged short stories, microwave ovens, and TV dinners. We want to

32

have it all and have it all now. An anonymous litany declares:

> This is the age of the half-read page,
> the mad dash, the quick hash,
> the lamp tan in a short span,
> the bright lights, the nerves tight,
> the plane hop, the brief stop,
> till the spring snaps and the fun's done.

Paul's word to Timothy, his son in the ministry, is a word of encouragement and challenge to us who desire to grow in grace. He writes, "Take strength from the grace of God which is ours in Christ Jesus" (2 Timothy 2:1, NEB). This strength enables us to express faithfulness in this relationship of trust. Note the different images used by Paul to help Timothy see the dimensions of his discipleship.

Obedience

Discipleship involves sacrifice and obedience, like the "good soldier" who takes on suffering. A soldier on active service is "wholly at (the) commanding officer's disposal" (2 Timothy 2:3-4, NEB).

Such a commitment includes our willingness to take risks and move out in faith. The children of Israel wandered in the wilderness for forty years. As they approached the promised land, Moses, their liberator, had died, and Joshua, their new leader, called them together. He spoke of the journey which they had already made. He reminded them of the way they had traveled thus far. He revealed that in all of the way, God was with them. God gave them a cloud by day and a pillar of fire by night. Now at the edge of the Jordan River, they are poised, ready to enter the land flowing with milk and honey. At this moment, Joshua speaks the word and challenges, "You have not passed this way before. . . . Sanctify yourselves; for tomorrow the Lord will do wonders among you" (Joshua 3:4-5). The next day, the people, behind their leader, step into the water toward the promised life.

Faith involves getting our feet wet. Discipleship includes the risk of stepping out in obedience to the rules of God. We are called to act out our obedience. The stories of persons who live out this life of obedience inspire all people, such as Mother Teresa, Dietrich Bonhoeffer, and Martin Luther King, Jr. Countless thousands of persons, whose names are known only to God, have been willing to take the same risk of obedience.

Paul tells Timothy, "Again, no athlete can win a prize unless [one] has kept the rules" (2 Timothy 2:5, NEB). Discipline is necessary to compete. A person must play by the rules and train if he or she expects to compete. Growing in this grace requires faithful discipline.

A third image is used of the hard-working farmer who enjoys the harvest. Remember the parable that Jesus tells of the farmer who sows his seed and then who waits for the seed to germinate, grow, and develop first. At the appropriate time, the farmer applies the sickle to the harvest. The story of Jesus is a great encouragement which reminds us of the reality of the kingdom now and the fullness of the kingdom to come. God does what God is to do, and the farmer does his work. Then comes the harvest. The persistent, confident, and patient farmer enjoys the harvest!

Remember, it is the grace of God working in us which makes it possible for us to work out. It is the spirit which makes us strong in our inner life (Ephesians 3:16). No amount of work can put us right with God. This is only possible through the grace of God. Grace continues to work in us enabling us to grow in grace. We are called to continually respond in trust and obedience to this grace. We may resist this tenacious and tender grace at any time in our journey. A mark of growing in grace is being zealous of good works. John Wesley states that if one willingly neglects work, one cannot expect to mature in the faith. (See Outler, *Works of John Wesley*, V. 2, "Scriptural Way of Salvation," p. 65.) Again, these good works are not the way to salvation, but the result of our being put in a right relationship with God in Christ.

Means of grace

What are the good works we must practice? What are some of the specific exercises that we must do to grow in grace? We are not left alone. The community of faith offers "means of grace" to help us grow in grace. For Wesley, these specific signs, words, and actions are ordained of God, whereby God might convey to persons the seeking, saving, and growing

35

grace of God. Wesley does not believe that these means are the only ways God bestows grace upon us, but they are several specific means by which God does work. And they are only means; they are not an end. In fact, Wesley says that when the means are separated from the end, the means are vanity. These means are channels through which God's grace flows into our lives, enabling us to grow in grace. (See Outler, *Works of John Wesley*, "Means of Grace," V. 1, pp. 378-97.)

Prayer.   *Prayer* is a means of grace. We cannot grow in our experience and relationship with God unless we spend time in the presence of God. God is always with us, but we must will to be present with God. Wesley states it plainly:

> All who desire the grace of God are to wait for it in the way of *prayer.* This is the express direction of our Lord himself. In his Sermon on the Mount, after explaining at large wherein religion consists, and describing the main branches of it, he adds: "Ask, and it shall be given you; seek, and ye shall find; knock, and it shall be opened unto you. For everyone that asketh, receiveth; and he that seeketh, findeth; and to him that knocketh, it shall be opened." Here we are in the plainest manner directed to ask in order to, or as a *means* of, receiving; to seek in order to find the grace of God, the pearl of great price; and to knock, to continue asking and seeking, if we would enter into his kingdom.[3]

We can immerse ourselves in the language of prayer

by reading the prayers of others and prayers in the psalms. We are called to practice private prayer—alone and in solitude. We need the experience of public prayer and of family prayers.

A disciplined prayer life is difficult to maintain. Yet, the life of the spirit is within to help us, to motivate us. I understand this motivation in the life of a friend who walks three miles every day, rain or shine, summer or winter. Since I easily shrink away from my routines of exercise, I asked my friend if it is difficult to keep the commitment to exercise by walking three miles every day.

"No! Not after the doctor explained it," he said.

"How's that?" I asked.

"The doctor told me, 'Walk or die.' So, I walk."

Prayer, for the disciple, is a matter of life or death. This discipline is necessary for spiritual breath. We learn to pray by expressing adoration and praise to God. We talk and listen to the Lord concerning the directions and petitions in our lives. Grace-esteem, the life of grace, requires prayer—regularly, systematically, spontaneously, and deeply. The deep craving for the renewing life in the Spirit of God is experienced in prayer.

Searching the scriptures. Those who desire to grow in the grace of God are to search the scriptures faithfully and diligently. Jesus informed his listeners that the scriptures bear witness to him (John 5:39). The scripture provides for each disciple a means of grace which leads to faith. In Paul's journey, the people at Beroea were opened to his message, and many of

37

them believed his word, for the people were "studying the scriptures every day" (Acts 17:11, NEB). Paul reminded Timothy that since "you were a child you have known the Holy Scriptures, which are able to give you the wisdom that leads to salvation through faith in Christ Jesus" (2 Timothy 3:15, TEV). Paul reinforces the importance of the scriptures for this young disciple:

> All Scripture is inspired by God and is useful for teaching the truth, rebuking error, correcting faults, and giving instruction for right living, so that the (person) who serves God may be fully qualified and equipped to do every kind of good work.
>
> (2 Timothy 3:16-17, TEV)

Without the regular exercise of searching the scriptures, we will grow flabby and weak in our spiritual life. The scriptures are important in leading us to faith and enabling us to do ministry and service in the name of Christ.

Many persons in our society and even in our churches are unaware of the message of the scripture. In the USA a man shows up at many sporting events, carrying a sign that reads "John 3:16." Surely everyone knows the meaning of John 3:16, you would think, but a letter to the editor of a popular magazine asked what the sign means. Obviously, some people in our land do not know the stories of fatih and need to hear the message.

For the disciple, regular study of the scripture, both private and public, is a necessity. Some ongoing, systematic study of the scripture is needed as much as food—meat, vegetables, fruit, and bread. A balanced diet for growing in grace-esteem includes meditation on the scriptures.

> Break thou the bread of life,
>   dear Lord to me,
> As thou didst break the loaves,
>   beside the sea.
> Beyond the sacred page,
>   I seek thee, Lord.
> My spirit pants for thee, O Living Word.
>   (*The United Methodist Hymnal,* 599)

The Lord's Supper.   Wesley preached to his hearers that "all who desire an increase of the grace of God are to wait for it in partaking of the Lord's Supper."[4] For Wesley it greatly mattered that Jesus commanded his followers to eat in remembrance of him. When we share the cup of blessing, we are sharing in the blood of Christ, and when we share the bread, we are sharing in the body of Christ (1 Corinthians 10:16). These are outward and visible means through which God pours into our hearts the grace and power of Christ Jesus. As we partake of this holy sacrament, we are keenly aware of our deep and continuing thirst to know God. Growing grace flows through the means of the Lord's Supper.

Fasting.   A fourth means of grace is fasting. John Wesley suggests that this is the most abused and the most neglected of all the means of grace. Some persons make it an end in itself, as if it were everything. Some persons treat it as if it were nothing. Wesley proposes that the truth is somewhere in between. Many of us in the Methodist tradition ignore this discipline. Could we be open to this means of grace to strengthen us in our discipleship? There are some important dimensions of the discipline for Wesley:

First fasting should be done unto the Lord. In the time of fasting, fix our eyes on the Lord and let the purpose be to glorify God.

Second, all who fast should understand that we do not do this to gain merit with God. God has promised to bless us freely. We are not negotiating with God by fasting.

> Let every season, either public or private fasting, be a season of exercising all those holy affections which are implied in a broken and contrite heart.[5]

Finally, fasting should be joined with fervent and earnest prayer. We should also pray for and do works of mercy to others. The commitment and discipline to fasting, indeed, can be a means whereby God pours out the Holy Spirit upon us as the people of God.

Christian fellowship. Every Christian must be a part of a true *koinonia* (fellowship) to grow and develop as a strong and faithful disciple. The early Christians were formed into a community of faith. In this fellowship they experienced the power and presence of the Holy Spirit. The Holy Spirit came to a gathered community of people who knew the name and believed in Jesus. Look at that early fellowship: "They met constantly to hear the apostles teach, and to share the common life, to break bread, and to pray. A sense of awe was everywhere" (Acts 2:42-43a, NEB). Christian discipleship includes incorporation into the Body of Christ. There is no such thing as solitary Christian discipleship. We are relational. The relationship with God is personal indeed, but it is not private. To grow in grace, we must love God and neighbor. The community of faith provides the arena for us to experience a redeeming fellowship and to model such a reconciling community to the world. We never live the life of grace in isolation. The Spirit came to a gathered group who knew and trusted in the name of Jesus.

We need the experience of public worship in the church. We require the fellowship of a small group. There is no substitute for the diet of regular worship with the gathered community when we offer our praise, adoration, confession, and commitment to Almighty God.

In addition, we need to belong to a small fellowship group which will help us grow in faithful obedience.

The small group fellowship "became the primary instrument of early Methodist renewal."[6] Wesley believed that every disciple needed a small, intimate fellowship where he or she could share deep concern and receive support for the Christian life. The class meeting of a dozen people became the primary place for Christian nurture. The societies met weekly for Bible study, singing, and testimony. This experience provided a comprehensive design for discipleship.[7]

This dynamic process enabled converts to the faith to become disciples of Christ.

I need this kind of fellowship to support me in my commitment and journey of discipleship. I am aware of my need to exercise. I know when I do it best—when I make arrangements to walk with my wife at lunch. Now, if I have that date, I will keep it! The group fellowship is a means of grace since it helps us be accountable in our pilgrimage.

No magic is involved in the means of grace. They are a means to an end, and not an end in themselves. Wesley writes that there is no power if the means are separate from God. By all means, he says, "Seek God alone. . . . Give God all the praise. Let God in all things be glorified through Christ Jesus."[8]

We are not left alone. Our life is continually dependent upon God's grace—pursuing grace, forgiving grace, and growing grace. God provides for us growing and graceful lives.

Questions for discussion

1. The example is shared (p. 29) of grandparents who see their grandchildren for the first time after a long absence and notice their growth. Reflecting on your spiritual pilgrimage, if someone were to see you for the first time in four years, what would they notice as different about you? How have you grown spiritually? (List at least one way in which God's grace has made a change.)

2. On page 33 we hear again the story of God's people wandering in the desert, finally coming to the promised land, and needing the encouragement to step into water behind their new leader, to take a risk. Reflect on a time when you had to risk, to step "into the water" in obedience to God's will for your faith journey. When have you needed to be obedient and found it helpful to follow another who encouraged you in your faithfulness? When have you been that encourager for another?

3. The chapter speaks of spiritual disciplines as means of grace and as necessary for growth. These were both individual and communal. Share at least one way in which you have experienced a discipline as a means of growing grace—as an individual discipline, as a community discipline. What area, in terms of your individual discipline, needs most "work" for you? Share an experience of your participation in one of the disciplines when you knew God's presence or guidance in a significant way.

4. Reflect on the section related to *koinonia*, the fellowship and encouragement of the Christian community. Read and meditate on Acts 2:42-43a. How does this influence your commitment to the importance of Christians being incorporated into the life of the church?

Chapter IV
GRACE-FULL

The life of Christian discipleship is the life of grace. At every point in the journey we are recipients of grace. There is no place in the pilgrimage where one can say "that will be all the grace I will need, thank you." No. The grace of God pursues us and seeks us from the earliest time of our lives. This grace makes it possible for us to respond in trust and obedience. And grace is given to enable us to grow fully into the stature of Christ.

> And so we shall all come together to that oneness in our faith and in our knowledge of the Son of God; we shall *become mature (people),* reaching to the *very height of Christ's full stature.* Then we shall no longer be children. . . . Instead, by speaking the truth in a spirit of love, we must *grow up in every way* to Christ, who is the head. Under his control all the different parts of the body fit together, and the whole body is held together by every joint with which it is provided. So when each separate part works as it should, the *whole body grows and builds itself up through love.*
>
> (Ephesians 4:13-16, TEV, emphasis added)

The grace and love of God operative in us makes it possible to become mature and fully grown. We continually receive the undeserved favor and graciousness from God through Christ which calls for us to be and become a grace-full people.

Wesley links together the New Birth, growing in grace, the fullness of grace and holiness of heart and life.

> When we are born again, then our sanctification, our inward and outward holiness, begins. And thenceforward we are gradually to 'grow up in him who is our head.' . . . A child is born of a woman in a moment, or at least a very short time. Afterward he gradually and slowly grows till he attains the stature of a man. In like manner a child is born of God in a short time, if not in a moment. But it is by slow degrees that he afterward grows up to the measure of the full stature of Christ.[1]

As a trusting recipient of God's grace we are filled by grace and become a people full of grace, or grace-full people. In this new relationship of being put right, we continue to grow up into Christ.

A relationship is dynamic, not static. That is, a relationship continues to grow and develop; it does not remain the same. Between persons, as a relationship of love continues, two people may grow closer and closer together. It is possible for persons to grow so close together that thoughts, dreams, desires, hopes, and aims all become intertwined. By grace, a relationship is established between God and us, with one another, and with creation. In this covenant of grace and trust, we are assured that we are forgiven. In a secure and assured relationship, it is possible to grow and mature in Christ.

Assurance

The assurance that Christ has forgiven our sins is pivotal in the life of John and Charles Wesley. With diligence and methodical activity the Wesleys sought to live holy lives during their days at Oxford University. John Wesley sought to be obedient to the utmost. He journeyed to North America seeking to be a missionary for God. He returned to England disappointed, thinking himself a failure. On this missionary journey he met Moravian brothers and sisters who were calm even in the midst of a ferocious storm. He questioned his own faith and doubted his relationship with God.

It was a discouraged and despondent man who entered St. Paul's Cathedral on May 24, 1738 for the evensong. When the anthem, "Out of the Depths I Cried," was sung it expressed Wesley's inner thoughts. Later that same evening, he went "very unwillingly" to a prayer meeting on Aldersgate Street. Wesley listened to the reading of Luther's preface to the Epistle of Romans and something happened in his life. He recorded his experience in his diary.

> About a quarter before nine, while he was describing the change which God works in the heart through faith in Christ, I felt my heart strangely warmed. I felt I did trust in Christ, Christ alone for

47

salvation: And an assurance was given me, that he had taken away *my* sins, even *mine,* and saved me from the law of sin and death.[2]

The key word is *assurance.* An assurance is given that even "my sins are taken away." This is a critical turning point in Wesley's life. His trust is now in what Christ has done and is doing for him. Before Aldersgate, he had focused more on what he was doing for God. This is a turning point for him. There was much before and much after, but here was the realization and awareness that he is forgiven.

It is possible to know that we are forgiven, not because of our goodness but because of God's graciousness. The Holy Spirit comes to assure us that we are indeed the children of God. In such a relationship we can mature and grow up grace-full.

The positive image and knowledge of being sons and daughters of God sparks a maturing development in the relationship with Christ. Charles Wesley wrote indeed, "How happy every child of grace who *knows* his sins forgiven." This does not mean that we are free from trouble. It does not mean that we are never disturbed, afraid, or lonely. It means that we know that each step of the way on our journey we are in the company of Jesus. We know we are living under the reign of grace. Indeed, this is enough for us.

Again let me emphasize that this assurance is not based on what I achieve. As Steve Harper says, "True assurance is not saying 'Look what a great Christian I am.' Rather it is saying 'Look at what a great Savior I have.' Here is the point of assurance—Christ has powerfully entered our lives, and it is his intention to stay."[3]

God in Christ has not only the power to forgive our sin, but also the power to give us a new life as we participate in the community of faith.

Walking in grace

Because of this new relationship, it is possible for us to live a new life, a life of grace-esteem. We can walk closely and constantly with Christ.

In the Bible we read that Enoch "walked with God" (Genesis 5:24). He just walks with God. He is no four-minute miler; he does not even jog. He just walks with God. That is his testimony and this experience reflects God's intent for humankind. In creation, God desired to walk in the cool of the day with Adam and Eve (Genesis 3:8).

Often the Bible describes this journey with God as one of walking:

"walking in newness of life" (Romans 6:4)

"we walk by faith" (2 Corinthians 5:7)

"walk in love, as Christ loved us and gave himself up for us (Ephesians 5:2)

"Look carefully then how you walk" (Ephesians 5:15)

"Walk by the Spirit" (Galatians 5:16)

49

To walk is to be going somewhere. It is to be active. To walk together is to share a common direction and destiny. Walking together involves sharing company. In this journey of trust and obedience, we know joy. We express this when we sing the gospel hymn

> Trust and obey.
> For there's no other way
> to be happy in Jesus,
> but to trust and obey.

(*The United Methodist Hymnal,* 467)

There is joy in loving God and following the commandments of God together. Again, we do not keep these commandments to get God to pardon us. God has already done that for us through Christ. We are forgiven and accepted by grace. Wesley wrote

> And now we are "alive to God, through Jesus Christ our Lord" (Romans 6:11). But we rejoice in walking according to the *covenant of grace,* in holy love and happy obedience. . . . through the power of his spirit freely given in Christ Jesus we also work the works of God.[4]

Walking in the covenant of grace is to live our lives under the rule of grace. The Lord's Supper is given to those who respond affirmatively to a very clear invitation of "walking from henceforth in God's holy ways."

Holy living

We are called to live holy lives. Grace can so fill our lives that we may live and walk in the way of the Spirit.

Just as the grace of God is active in our conversion, so the grace of God continues to enable us to become fully mature. Grace makes holiness of heart and life possible. If holiness is not rooted in grace, the disciplined life is characterized by elitism. Holiness is grace-full, never legalistic. Paul, writing to the Corinthians, said, "When I *grew* up I had finished with childish things" and became a mature person (1 Corinthians 13:11, NEB).

John Wesley continually called the people to a life of holiness. He believed that by grace one could be perfected in love. He did not see Christian perfection as that which is spiritually "superior" or as a person who is free from mistakes or temptations.[5] Rather, perfection is living so closely to and breathing the Spirit of God that we live in the Spirit and walk by the Spirit. It is living each and every day, not by our own merits and strengths but by the grace of God.

The mark of this grace-full life is the love of God and love of neighbors. It is singleness of intent and desire. We are not able to perform perfectly, but by God's grace, our desires and intent can be cleansed.

Our love may be pure, but we make grave errors in expressing it. For example, imagine a very hot day. A mother and father are working outside in the garden. As they look up, they notice their five-year-old daughter heading toward them. In her hands she carries a glass which contains a liquid. Obviously, she is bringing them a drink of cool water to refresh them in their work. As the little girl comes closer, they notice that she has three dirty fingers inside the glass, and there are brown streaks flowing down into the water.

She offers them the drink, saying, "Mommy and Daddy, I love you." Of course, the parents will take the glass and drink from it! The motive is of genuine love, though the expression and performance are far from perfect.

Love to God. God's grace sees our hearts and our motives. God knows our hearts' desires. Wesley sees that the essence of God's grace working in our hearts is that of deepening our love to God. The primary question is the same as Jesus asked of Simon Peter—Do you *love* me? Do you *love* me? Do you *love* me? (John 21:15-17, NEB). This is the heart of the matter. It is God's grace which makes this love to God possible.

The image of God is found within us and contains the gift to love. Henri Nouwen wrote that "what makes us human is not our mind, but our heart, not our ability to think, but our ability to love."[6] By God's grace this image is restored, and we may increasingly love God. The wonderful word is that we, by God's grace, *can* love and, therefore, by God's grace we *must* love. First and above all else, holiness means love to God.

Love to neighbor. Our love is to God and our love is to neighbor. The grace-full life is gracious toward neighbors. The work of grace enables us to be gracious and grace-full. It is interesting to note that the first act or thought of Wesley when he felt his heart strangely warmed was to begin to "pray with all my might for those who had in a more especial manner despitefully used me and persecuted me."[7]

This love for neighbor is often in conflict with the world. Our world teaches us how to dominate others. We are told how to intimidate or manipulate others. We are given training on how to get to the top of the pyramid. We want to be the lead dog in the pack because we learn early that only the lead dog has a changing view of the scenery! But the life possessed by grace and filled with gratitude sees the world with different eyes. Jesus gave us a different picture of one who is willing to serve and care for others even when it is costly. Jesus is not talking about debasing ourselves (in fact, we are to have a healthy love of self), but acting out of genuine love for others. In a world that is increasingly confident that power and might is the way to relate to others, we who are "graced" know a better way.

The grace-full life is one that serves in such a way that God's grace is manifested to others. Out of a sense of gratitude for what God has done and is doing for us, we love and give ourselves for others. God cares for us and, therefore, we care for others. We love others and we see God. This love fills us with compassion for others; as the moving line in *Les Misérables* says, "To love another is to see the face of God."

Compassion and love for others is a mark of the grace-full life. Freda and Abel Hendricks of South Africa know and live their lives of grace. They are people who exemplify the love and care for neighbor. Under their leadership, the church has increased significantly in membership and ministry in the community. Abel has suffered with his people as they seek to throw off the shackles of a system which oppresses the people. On more than one occasion, he had been imprisoned for responsibilities he carried out in ministering with his people.

One day as Freda and Abel were traveling through their area, they heard some children crying. They made their way over to the edge of the road and noticed some children looking for food in a garbage dump. They asked each child about his or her parents and discovered that there was no one who cared for the children. Abel and Freda wept and fell to their knees in the garbage dump and promised God that as long as "we live in this community no child will look for bread in a garbage dump again!" They promised God! Today, several hundred children in daycare centers across their area are given warm meals each day—all because of love to God and love to neighbor.

Love and justice. Love to God is expressed outwardly and visibly in love to neighbor. We see and know that we are made in the image of God. Grace makes it possible to see others as precious and valuable. This grace helps me to see myself as worth something and to see others as persons of great worth. The essence of justice is the restoration and reinforcement of a God-given dignity to every person. Injustice is done when we fail to see the image of God in others and treat people as worthless. A story is told about a young man who became a cipher—a zero—because of the way he was treated by others. In the story, Cliff, a young elementary school student, died suddenly and without apparent cause. His death perplexed the school. Cliff's favorite teacher was especially shocked.

As he investigated, he discovered that no one in the school knew Cliff or remembered him. Cliff's home life offered little relief or encouragement. Cliff belonged to no clubs or teams. The teacher discovered that the young boy had been made a zero by others—family, classmates, and teachers. He was told "you are nothing" by so many people so often that he became a cipher and died. Because of this experience, the teacher promised himself that every student in his class would be treated like a somebody. He also promised that he would seek those who felt worthless and make them feel like somebody too.[8]

A mark of those who receive the grace of God is loving others and helping others discover their "dot on the king's map." It is possible for persons to grow up with a distorted view of themselves. It is like looking in a curved mirror at the county fair. We get a funny image of ourselves. We have a warped view of who we are. Loving and caring for others helps people discover their true worth and value. Unless someone cares, people miss knowing that they are children of God.

We are called genuinely to love others. We find ourselves struggling with injustice that enslaves others. We know that if there are others anywhere who are enslaved, we ourselves are enslaved. If everybody is not welcome into the home of the Lord, then no one is welcome. Righteousness involves engaging the powers which dehumanize people. One of the most dramatic decisions in the life of Wesley was when he decided (again, reluctantly) to go into the open air and marketplace to share the good news with common people. In some ways this is the decision which gave rise to the whole Methodist movement. He said that he consented to speak with the people who had been marginalized by his society. The message of grace—that you are somebody, a child of God—penetrated the hearts of the people in Wesley's day. The faces of the people were streaked with tears of joy in coming to know that God's grace is for them. Out of this compassion for people, Wesley developed ministries with homeless children and the poor. This ministry to the people was the result of the Aldersgate experience in Wesley's life.

This compassion for others is rooted in love to God. Social righteousness is rooted in deep spirituality. The grace of God works in our heart to enable us to love God and neighbor. Henri Nouwen states that "by heart I do not mean the seat of human emotions in contrast to the mind as the seat of human thought. No, by heart I mean the center of our being where God has hidden the divine gifts of trust, hope and love. . . . The heart allows us to enter into relationships and become sons and daughters of God, and brothers and sisters of each other."[9]

Gifts of ministry

The gifts and fruit of the Spirit-filled and grace-full life come out of the center of our being, the heart. The gifts of the Spirit and the fruit of the Spirit are closely intertwined. In fact, the gifts are given for ministry and the fruit is the harvest of the Spirit-filled life. Both the gifts and the fruit of the Spirit are the result of the grace of God working in us.

The gifts of the Spirit are all gifts of ministry. The Spirit is not given to the people of God so that we may feel good, but that in the name of the Lord Jesus Christ we do ministry.

The gifts of ministry are all different, not superior or inferior. The gifts of the Spirit are given for the good of the whole body. Paul said that it is ridiculous for a body to try to function with only one part. Can you imagine trying to live as only an eye? Or an elbow? So it is in the gifts of ministry. They are given for the good of all as needed and as the Spirit decides.

> It is one and the same Spirit who does all this; he gives a different gift to each (person), as he wishes.

> (1 Corinthians 12:11, TEV)

The gifts are given by grace, and they are given to be put to use. They are not for our sake but for the whole church and for the sake of others. "As each has received a gift, employ it for one another, as good stewards of God's varied *grace* ... that in everything God may be glorified through Jesus Christ" (1 Peter 4:10-11).

The gifts of ministry flow outward from an inward work of grace. The gifts are given as needed which means that some particular gift of ministry may not be given us for a lifetime but for a particular situation.

The Spirit is poured out upon us to do ministry in the name of the one who calls us. Charles Wesley wrote,

57

To serve the present age
    my calling to fulfill
O may it my powers engage
    to do my master's will.
(*The United Methodist Hymnal*, 413)

The master's vision of ministry is our call:

The spirit of the Lord is upon me because he has
    annointed me;
He has sent me to announce good news to the
    poor,
To proclaim release for prisoners and recovery of
    sight for the blind;
To let the broken victims go free,
To proclaim the year of the Lord's favour.
(Luke 4:18, NEB)

The gifts of ministry given by the Spirit enable the church to live out this vision in the world.

The very famous painting by Holman Hunt pictures Jesus standing and knocking at the door. I recently stood in St. Paul's Cathedral and studied the painting. There is no doorknob outside, which means that the door must be opened from the inside. Jesus is holding a light in his hand, illuminating all the surroundings. He is patiently and persistently knocking. I know the promise that if I open he will come into my heart and life. But I also know that he beckons me to follow him in faithful discipleship in the world. Perhaps he knocks not to come in, but that I will come out into the streets to minister in his name.

Each "graced" person is given the gifts of ministry.

We can become increasingly aware of the gifts that God bestows on us, and we can encourage others to discover and develop these gifts of grace.

Harvest of grace

Following the discourse on the gifts of ministry, Paul writes, "And I will show you a still more excellent way" (1 Corinthians 12:31). He shows the way of love which is the ultimate expression of the life which is full of grace and maturing in the Spirit. The Spirit leads us to the best way. Our hearts, the center of being, are transformed, and the Spirit produces the harvest.

The harvest of the Spirit is experienced intensely inward and expressed vigorously outward. Our hearts are cleansed; out of this grace-filled life flow the expressions and evidences of love. The center of our life needs this transforming grace. Don English tells an old English story about a town which received its water from one well. The well began producing dirty water. A town council convened to consider the situation. An old man attempted to speak, but he was told, "We will hear you later." Someone observed, "We have not told the well how important it is." Thinking that a show of appreciation would help, the townspeople decorated the well; but the water still came out dirty. The townspeople decided to remind the well of its responsibility; but the water still came out dirty. Again, at a council meeting, the old man tried to speak, but he was told, "No. Wait and we will come to you." Meanwhile, a teacher tried a show of force; but the water still came out dirty. Finally, the council listened to the old man.

"Out of the heart proceed evil deeds and wicked thoughts," the man said. "These are they which defile a person. Look at the heart of the well and see what has gone wrong."

Some townspeople descended into the well and discovered a dead cat which had been contaminating the water all along. Once the cat was removed, the water ran clean again.[10]

It is a simple but profound message that the grace of God moves to touch at the center of our being. The maturing work of grace is deep within us, enabling us to be a grace-full people. By God's grace, we continue to grow up into the measure of fullness in Christ.

The Christ-like qualities all began at the center of our being. Paul, in writing to the Galatians, helps us to see the fruit of the Spirit.

> The harvest of the Spirit is love, joy, peace, patience, kindness, goodness, fidelity, gentleness, and self-control. . . . If the Spirit is the source of our life, let the Spirit also direct our course.
>
> (Galatians 5:22-25, NEB)

Out of the relationship of trust, the Spirit produces the fruit of the Spirit: LOVE. A grace-full person is possessed by the desire to live the way of love. It is the more excellent way. A paraphrasing of 1 Corinthians 13 by a group of young persons gives us an interesting picture of the way of love. (The words may differ, but the ideas are the same as Paul's on the way of love.)

60

If I can sing 'Green Grow the Rushes Ho' from
      memory or preach like Billy Graham,
      but say nothing loving,
      I am nothing but an electric guitar or a set of
      drums.
If I have ESP and am learned as Einstein or can
      blow up Camp Montgomery by the exertion
      of faith alone,
      but have no love in my heart,
      I am as empty as outer space.
If I put my whole wardrobe in the Goodwill box
      or set myself afire like a Buddhist monk,
      but do them without love,
      I accomplish exactly zero.

Love does not lose its cool. It is thoughtful of
      others' feelings.
Love is not a green-eyed monster,
      nor is it like the little girl in Charlie Brown
      with the naturally curly hair.
Love is not snobbish and forms no cliques.
It is not rude, crude and unattractive.
It does not insist on its own way like Lucy does in
      "Peanuts."
Love is not like parents before they have had their
      morning coffee.
Love does not feel the same way I do when a
      teacher asks a question on the final that has
      never been discussed in class.
Love does not spread untrue gossip, but instead is
      glad to have it squashed.
Love has put up with the group's pranks this week.

Love trusts in the strengths and righteousness of
    God.
It sees the doughnut and not the hole.
Love puts up with small irritations constantly.

Love is for keeps.
As for ouija boards, political speeches, and
    Ph.D.'s, they will croak.
Our data is incomplete, and the tea leaves some-
    times lie.
But when love reigns, war, hunger, and strife will
    end.
When I was a kid I talked baby talk;
    my thoughts were immature.
    My reasoning was for the birds.
But when I grew up, I began to mature.
As long as we are trapped inside these human
    bodies, we can only partially understand the
    wonders of the universe,
        but one day God's knowledge will be ours,
        and we will know him as completely as he
        knows us.
So faith, hope, and love will last forever,
    but I'll put *my* money on *love.*[11]

The fruit of the maturing, grace-full life reflects these
qualities and characteristics of love. The grace of God
is given for us in the death and resurrection. Evil,
hatred, and sin have no right to control us as individuals, churches, communities, or nations. We do not
have to say "Well, that is just my temper or my
attitude, or my habit or my sin." We can be set free
and cleansed so that sin no longer reigns in our lives.

Grace transforms our hearts and lives, and we live the way of love.

Each disciple is given the power to witness to this transforming grace in our lives. We are called to communicate this grace by word and deed in our community and with our neighbors. There is a time for us to declare intentionally and faithfully the reason we have hope within us. In living the way of love, we share verbally and lovingly what God is doing in our lives. We are given the power to live a grace-full life. The Spirit produces a harvest of the Spirit and the power to witness in the Spirit.

Grace and hope

Through many dangers, toils and snares
    I have already come;
'Tis grace hath brought me safe thus far,
And grace will lead me home.
(The United Methodist Hymnal, 378)

The grace of God makes possible this new being and new relationship with God, others, and the whole universe. The work of grace makes possible a new life and whole new order (2 Corinthians 5:17). This relationship of wholeness (very close to holiness) begins in the reconciling work of Christ and the continuing work of grace within us. By grace and our response of trust, we grow closer and closer to Christ now. Death does not alter that relationship. The grace of God is given to all, but it is not irresistible. The response of faith and trust is necessary for one to enter into the eternal life of grace. For Wesley, the presence of the kingdom demands decision. It is a sobering reality to choose to live in darkness rather than in the light.[12]

By grace through faith we move into the realm of wholeness and the kingdom of light. Once we saw only partially, but now we can see fully this reign of grace. Grace gives us hope because when we look through the corridors of time and space, we see that the future is open. We know that one day God's kingdom will fully come. We are motivated by the vision of a future when God's rule is complete.

Replays of the University of Tennessee basketball games are sometimes televised after the last newscast of the evening. The final score is available during the newscast for those who don't plan to watch the replay. I always want to see the score first because I will not watch if Tennessee loses. I want to know how it comes out at the end.

Similarly, we are given a vision of what it is like when God's rule of grace is established. Grace helps us to remember from whence we come, and grace gives us a vision of what God has promised. For those who by grace choose to live in terms of God's grace, death does not break or sever the relationship. Our present life by grace is the pathway into the fuller realm of glory.

One person who is a great witness to this obedient journey of discipleship in life and death is Dietrich Bonhoeffer. His life reflected this grace-full living, and his death witnessed to his hope and confidence for the future.

The time was April 9th, 1945. The prison doctor at Flossenburg wrote this report: "On the morning of the day, some time between five and six o'clock the prisoners . . . were led out of their cells and the verdicts read to them. Through the half-open door of a room in one of the huts I saw Pastor Bonhoeffer, still in his prison clothes, kneeling in fervent prayer to the Lord his God. The devotion and evident conviction of being heard that I saw in the prayer of this intensely captivating man, moved me to the depths." So the morning came. Now the prisoners were ordered to strip. They were led down a little flight of steps under the trees to the secluded place of execution. There was a pause. . . . Naked under the scaffold in the sweet spring woods, Bonhoeffer knelt for the last time to pray. Five minutes later, his life was ended. . . . Three weeks later Hitler committed suicide. In another month the Third Reich had fallen. All Germany was in chaos and communications were impossible. No one knew what had happened to Bonhoeffer. His family waited in anguished uncertainty in Berlin. The report of his death was first received in Geneva and then telegraphed to England. On July 27th his aged parents, as was their custom, turned on their radio to listen to the broadcast from London. A memorial service was in progress. The triumphant measures of Vaughan Williams' "For All The Saints" rolled out loud and solemn from many hundred voices. Then a single German was speaking in English, "We are gathered here in the presence of God to make thankful remembrance of the life and work of his servant Dietrich Bonhoeffer, who gave his life in faith and obedience to His holy word."[13]

Bonhoeffer's life and death were grounded in the abounding grace of God. In Christ we too can live in the present and in the world to come.

We can by grace come to face our life and our death with the words of affirmation spoken by Wesley on his death bed, "The best of all is—God is with us." By grace we may abide in Christ now and into the future. Paul, in writing to the Philippians, states that the spiritually mature

> run straight toward the goal in order to win the prize, which is God's call through Christ Jesus to the life above.
>
> (Philippians 3:14-15, TEV)

The secret

There is a secret how we may know the fullness of all that we are created and intended to be. We may know that we are indeed a "graced" people. We not only have our dots on the king's map, we are a "royal priesthood...and God's own people." Once we "were no people but now (we) are God's people. Once (we) had not received mercy but now (we) have received mercy" (1 Peter 2:9-10).

God wants to transform and conform us into the image of God. How is it possible? We *yield* our lives to the power of the indwelling Christ. At one time I used the word *surrender,* but I developed a problem with it because of my past. I have a brother two years older than I am. As we were growing up, I remember that we often engaged in wrestling matches. It usually ended with my brother on top of me saying "Surrender! Say 'I give.'"

"No!"

"Surrender!"

"No!" I could not say it. If I said "surrender," I would be destroyed. I would be a nobody. I would have no dignity left. When I hear the word *surrender* I see the face of my brother. I found another word, *yield.* (It means the same, but it involves no hang-ups.) To yield my life to the amazing grace of Jesus is not to be wiped out or destroyed. No. I am forgiven and empowered to become what God created me to be. The grace of God comes persistently and patiently (but not irresistibly) to meet you and me at every intersection of our lives. This wonderful grace of Jesus comes to us at every junction and juncture of our journey.

Paul, in writing to the Colossians, declares, "The secret is this: Christ in you, the hope of a glory to come" (Colossians 1:27, NEB). This is our hope of being a new creation and growing in full maturity. We *may* live by grace in this life and the one to come. The secret of grace-esteem is that Christ dwells within us! Yielding by grace to the indwelling Christ is to be given the power to live new, whole, grace-full lives.

The 250th anniversary of Aldersgate was celebrated May 24, 1988. At a great service in St. Paul's Cathedral in London, more than 2,500 people from 90 countries gathered to offer praise to God and the Lord Jesus

Christ. The ecumenical service included the Archbishop of Canterbury and the President of the World Methodist Council. Her Majesty, Queen Elizabeth, and Prince Phillip gathered to thank God for the faithful witness of the Wesleys more than 200 years ago. My wife and I were only a few seats away from the reigning monarch; therefore, we were excited throughout the service. I could not help but feel the prayerful participation of the queen and all the people. The climax of the service came when we stood to sing one of the greatest Wesleyan hymns. The queen did not even have to look at the words. She sang the hymn by heart! The hymn she sang summarizes the secret and center of our faith. It is the appropriate prayer for us and we are invited to sing and pray it again:

Love divine, all loves excelling,
Joy of heaven to earth come down;
Fix in us thy humble dwelling;
All thy faithful mercies crown!
Jesus, thou art all compassion,
Pure, unbounded love thou art;
Visit us with thy salvation;
Enter every trembling heart.

Breathe, O breathe thy living spirit
Into every troubled breast!
Let us all in thee inherit;
Let us find that second rest.
Take away our bent to sinning;
Alpha and Omega be;
End of faith, as its beginning,
Set our hearts at liberty.

Come, Almighty to deliver,
Let us all thy life receive;
Suddenly return and never,
Nevermore thy temples leave.
Thee we would be always blessing,
Serve thee as thy hosts above,
Pray and praise thee without ceasing,
Glory in thy perfect love.

Finish, then, thy new creation;
Pure and spotless let us be.
Let us see thy great salvation
Perfectly restored in thee:
Changed from glory into glory,
Till in heaven we take our place,
Till we cast our crowns before thee,
Lost in wonder, love, and praise.
                    Amen.

(*The United Methodist Hymnal*, 384)

Questions for discussion

1. In speaking of assurance (p. 47) and being perfected in love (p. 51), we see the reality of our life in
   Christ, which is enabling our lives to be grace-full,
   yet not promising our lives will be free of trouble, or
   pain, or disease. Assurance, rather, speaks to God's
   presence with us in the journey. How does this fit
   with your own experience, or the experience of
   persons around you, or the experience of persons

of great faith in oppressive situations? What is the difference between thinking we can "make it on our own" and having the assurance that we know God's forgiving and sustaining love in Christ?

2. What are the ways in which you express your love to God?
   a. Note the response of Wesley (p. 47) following his experience of the "warmed heart." When did you last feel moved to pray for those who "persecuted you" or used you?
   b. In what ways do you share God's love for others as you are motivated by God's love for you?

3. What are your gifts for ministry? In what ways do you feel that you really are enabled to reach out to others, to serve and care for God's people?

4. Read again Colossians 1:27. What does that mean in your own life?

5. How have you experienced and known grace-esteem? What does that mean in your own life and as you love God by reaching out to others?

6. Is God "finishing the new creation" in you?

ENDNOTES

Chapter 2

1 Albert Outler, *The Works of John Wesley* V. 2 (Nashville: Abingdon, 1985), pp. 156-57.
2 Donald English, *The Meaning of the Warmed Heart* (Nashville: Discipleship Resources, 1987), pp. 3-4.
3 Maxie Dunnam, *Our Journey: A Wesleyan View of the Christian Way* (Nashville: Discipleship Resources, 1984), p. 16.
4 Albert Outler, *The Works of John Wesley* V. 2 (Nashville: Abingdon, 1985), p. 162.
5 David Seamands, *Healing for Damaged Emotions* (Wheaton, IL: Victor Books, 1987), p. 116.
6 Dunnam, *Our Journey,* p. 16.

Chapter 3

1 Outler, *The Works of John Wesley* V. 2, p. 158.
2 Ibid., p. 160.
3 Outler, *The Works of John Wesley* V. 1 (Nashville: Abingdon, 1984), p. 384.
4 Ibid., p. 389.
5 Ibid., pp. 609-11.
6 Steve Harper, *John Wesley's Message for Today*

(Grand Rapids, MI: Francis Asbury Press, 1983), p. 83.

7 Ibid., p. 84.

8 Outler, *The Works of John Wesley* V. 1, pp. 396-97.

Chapter 4

1 Outler, *The Works of John Wesley* V. 2, p. 198.

2 Thomas Jackson, *Wesley's Works* V. 1 (Grand Rapids, MI: Baker Book House, 1978), p. 103.

3 Harper, p. 77.

4 Outler, *The Works of John Wesley* V. 1, pp. 312-13.

5 Ibid., pp. 100-104.

6 Henri Nouwen, "The Peace That Is Not of This World," *Weavings* 3 (1988).

7 Jackson, *Wesley's Works,* V. 1, p. 103.

8 Joe Harding, *Have I Told You Lately?* (Pasadena: Church Growth Press, 1982), pp. 68-72.

9 Nouwen, pp. 28-29.

10 Donald English, unpublished lecture at Congress on Evangelism, January 1988, in Chicago, Illinois.

11 James L. Christensen, *New Ways to Worship* (Old Tappan, NJ: Fleming H. Revell Co., 1973), pp. 37-38.

12 Harper, pp. 110-12.

13 Eugene H. Peterson, *A Long Obedience in the Same Direction* (Downer's Grove, IL: InterVarsity Press, 1980), pp. 178-79.